Passengers
EIGHT SHORT PLAYS

by Sam Bobrick

NEW YORK HOLLYWOOD LONDON TORONTO

SAMUELFRENCH.COM

Copyright © 1984, 2008 by Sam Bobrick

ALL RIGHTS RESERVED

CAUTION: Professionals and amateurs are hereby warned that *PASSENGERS* is subject to a royalty. It is fully protected under the copyright laws of the United States of America, the British Commonwealth, including Canada, and all other countries of the Copyright Union. All rights, including professional, amateur, motion picture, recitation, lecturing, public reading, radio broadcasting, television and the rights of translation into foreign languages are strictly reserved. In its present form the play is dedicated to the reading public only.

The amateur live stage performance rights to *PASSENGERS* are controlled exclusively by Samuel French, Inc., and royalty arrangements and licenses must be secured well in advance of presentation. PLEASE NOTE that amateur royalty fees are set upon application in accordance with your producing circumstances. When applying for a royalty quotation and license please give us the number of performances intended, dates of production, your seating capacity and admission fee. Royalties are payable one week before the opening performance of the play to Samuel French, Inc., at 45 W. 25th Street, New York, NY 10010.

Royalty of the required amount must be paid whether the play is presented for charity or gain and whether or not admission is charged.

Stock royalty quoted upon application to Samuel French, Inc.

For all other rights than those stipulated above, apply to: Abrams Artists Agency, 275 Seventh Avenue, 26th Floor, New York, NY 10001 Attn: Ron Gwiazda.

Particular emphasis is laid on the question of amateur or professional readings, permission and terms for which must be secured in writing from Samuel French, Inc.

Copying from this book in whole or in part is strictly forbidden by law, and the right of performance is not transferable.

Whenever the play is produced the following notice must appear on all programs, printing and advertising for the play: "Produced by special arrangement with Samuel French, Inc."

Due authorship credit must be given on all programs, printing and advertising for the play.

ISBN 978-0-573-66267-6   Printed in U.S.A.   #19037

No one shall commit or authorize any act or omission by which the copyright of, or the right to copyright, this play may be impaired.

No one shall make any changes in this play for the purpose of production.

Publication of this play does not imply availability for performance. Both amateurs and professionals considering a production are strongly advised in their own interests to apply to Samuel French, Inc., for written permission before starting rehearsals, advertising, or booking a theatre.

No part of this book may be reproduced, stored in a retrieval system, or transmitted in any form, by any means, now known or yet to be invented, including mechanical, electronic, photocopying, recording, videotaping, or otherwise, without the prior written permission of the publisher.

IMPORTANT BILLING AND CREDIT REQUIREMENTS

All producers of *PASSENGERS* must give credit to the Author of the Play in all programs distributed in connection with performances of the Play, and in all instances in which the title of the Play appears for the purposes of advertising, publicizing or otherwise exploiting the Play and/or a production. The name of the Author *must* appear on a separate line on which no other name appears, immediately following the title and *must* appear in size of type not less than fifty percent of the size of the title type.

PASSENGERS requires only 4 actors, preferably a man and woman in their mid-forties to early fifties (Actors A and B) and another couple in their mid-late twenties (Actors C and D).

CHARACTERS IN ORDER OF APPEARANCE

ACT I

SCENE 1 - WAITING
Walter (Actor A)
Jane (B)
Howard (C)
Lorraine (D)

SCENE 2 - BABY FEET FRANK
Frank (C)
Clara (D)
Bus Driver (A)

SCENE 3 – OLD FRIENDS
Bag Lady (B)
Fred (A)

SCENE 4 – A BETTER WORLD
Audrey (D)
Ernest (A)
Marsha (B)
Al (C)

ACT II

SCENE 5 – HERE'S HARRY
Mrs. Evans (B)
Mr. Wade (A)

SCENE 6 – THE HAPPIEST BRIDE
Bobby (C)
June (D)

SCENE 7 – WITHOUT REGRETS
Mace (A)
Laura (B)

SCENE 8 – LAST BUS
June (D)
Al (C)
Mace (A)
Bag Lady (B)

ACT I

THE SET:

The entire play takes place in a small bus station. Stage Left are two sets of double doors leading to the street. Stage Right are two sets of double doors leading to the bus boarding area. Upstage Left Center is a caged ticket booth, the window obscure enough so that it is impossible to tell whether or not there is an occupant. Center Stage is a waiting bench. Another bench or two may be placed appropriately. There are the usual bus station posters on the wall, a coin operated sandwich machine, coffee dispenser, a trash can and a wall pay phone.

AT RISE:

(**JANE**, *a shy woman in her late-thirties and* **HOWARD**, *a man in his mid-thirties, are seated on the benches. Howard has a briefcase near him and is engrossed in a newspaper.* **WALTER**, *a man in his early forties, walks around pensively. He then goes to Howard*)

WALTER. Excuse me, but how long have we been dead?

HOWARD. What?

WALTER. How long have we been dead?

(**HOWARD** *turns away and continues to read the paper.* **WALTER** *goes to* **JANE**)

WALTER *(Continued)* I thought he would know.

JANE. Maybe you should have asked me.

WALTER. Do you know?

JANE. No, but I would have welcomed the dialogue. I didn't bring any reading material.

WALTER. Well, we're dead you know.

JANE. You really think so?

WALTER. We have to be. I mean, here I am in this bus station and I have no idea where I'm going.

JANE. I can see why you're concerned.

WALTER. You're not upset?

JANE. I don't know. I'd like to think about it for a bit.

WALTER. How long have you been waiting here?

JANE. It seems forever.

WALTER. It's all adding up, isn't it?

JANE. It could be.

WALTER. Well, it's adding up for me.

HOWARD. *(Lowering paper. To* **WALTER***)* Look, will you do me a favor?

WALTER. Sure.

HOWARD. On the bus, don't sit next to me.

WALTER. Okay.

HOWARD. Good.

WALTER. *(A beat)* What bus?

HOWARD. What?

WALTER. What bus?

HOWARD. What bus what?

WALTER. What bus are we waiting for?

HOWARD. Look at your ticket, you idiot.

WALTER. I don't have one.

HOWARD. Then buy one.

WALTER. To where?

HOWARD. To where ever you're going.

WALTER. I told you. I have no idea where I'm going.

HOWARD. Oh, hell.

WALTER. Oh, God, I hope not there.

HOWARD. *(Rising and indicating)* You stay here. I'm moving over there. Try to keep your voice down.

(He moves to the far end of the bench)

WALTER. You don't think we're dead?

HOWARD. I think you're sick.

WALTER. Well, I know I'm dead and you know something else? I feel real good about it.

(To **JANE**)

There are a lot of advantages in death. For one thing, I won't need haircuts anymore. I hate haircuts. Not so much the haircut itself, but the part at the end when the barber shaves your neck with a razor. I always feel I should know more about the mental condition of a man who has me in that position. What do you like about being dead?

JANE. Well, it seems you're much more extroverted. That's why I think you could be right, that we are dead. I have great difficulty approaching people. And when someone approaches me, you know, the way you just did, I usually feel I want to disappear right into my shoes.

WALTER. You're shy?

JANE. No. Socially retarded. I have to be honest with myself.

WALTER. I adore shy girls. I have a hunch they might be easier to please.

JANE. We are. We keep a lot inside.

WALTER. They say that's unhealthy.

JANE. I know. It could kill you, although if your theory of our expiration is correct that could be a redundant thought.

WALTER. Yes, maybe so.

JANE. You have a high forehead. I'll bet you're educated. Are you?

WALTER. I've had a year and a half of college.

JANE. I thought so.

WALTER. I would have gone farther but it really didn't seem necessary for the dental supply business. That's what I sold before the angel of death decided to step in.

HOWARD. *(Lowers paper and raises voice)* I can still hear you.

WALTER. What's that?

HOWARD. You're talking too loud. I can still hear you.

JANE. *(A deep breath)* We are in a bus station, sir, Not a library. We can speak as loudly as we want.

(**HOWARD**, *annoyed, returns to his paper*)

WALTER. Hey, that's good. That's real self-assertion for a socially retarded person.

JANE. Yes. Wasn't it? Did you like that in me? The strength I showed?

WALTER. Absolutely. If you don't stick up for yourself, who will?

JANE. True. But I really wasn't that comfortable. I know it's a disadvantage, but I actually prefer a softness in my manner of function.

WALTER. Yes. I like that more in an individual myself, but it's not very practical in today's society. Although why should we care about that anyway, now that we're in cloud city. Which brings up the question of everyday vernacular around here. I think it's bound to be a bit confusing for us at first. Do we say, "That's life!" Or "That was life"? Do we say, "That's the way it goes" or "That's the way it went"?

JANE. "What do you know?", or "What did you know?"

WALTER. Exactly. They must have rules for that here. I'll check.

(Loudly to ceiling)

Hi! Do you have rules for that?

HOWARD. You're out of your minds. You're both absolutely out of your minds. I don't know about you, but I'm alive! I just kissed my wife and kids goodbye. I'm not going to see them for three weeks. I feel wonderful.

WALTER. What is it you do?

HOWARD. I'm an insurance man.

WALTER. We may not be going to the same place.

HOWARD. Look, stop making me nuts, okay?

(Returns to paper)

WALTER. Okay.

(A beat. To **JANE**)

Did you leave behind any loved ones?

JANE. Yes. Half a cat. I shared him.

WALTER. With whom?

JANE. I don't know. Every now and then he would drop by. I would feed him, pet him, and he would sit by my chair and then just as suddenly as he appeared, he would disappear. I'd never see him go. I always felt that while he enjoyed my company at times, I couldn't completely fulfill him as a person.

WALTER. I have a cat too. But I have to admit, he makes me feel a little uncomfortable at times. Every once in a while I'll find him staring at me as if to say, Walter Cranston, ho hum.

JANE. *(A beat)* Some cats are very deep.

WALTER. It seems so.

JANE. Walter Cranston. I like that name. It sounds dignified, yet blameless. Is Mrs. Walter Cranston still among the living?

WALTER. Lorraine? I don't remember her being with me in my final moments. Gee, an existence without Lorraine. This could be heaven.

JANE. You weren't happy? Oh, I'm so glad.

(Puts her hand to her lips in embarrassment)

Oh, my goodness. Look how forward I've gotten. Oh, I enjoy being dead. I really do. It's such a wonderful approach to life.

HOWARD. *(Rising)* I can't take this anymore. Have either of you got two quarters.

WALTER. Sure, why?

HOWARD. I forgot my cell phone and I want to call my wife. She'll tell me whether I'm dead or not. Better yet, give me four quarters. Just in case I need a second opinion.

WALTER. *(Takes change from pocket and hands it to him)* Here! Take all my change. Apparently I'm not going to have any need for it now.

HOWARD. You both should be put away, you know that?

(He goes to the phone)

JANE. I feel so good, so free.

WALTER. Me, too. What did you do when you were alive?

JANE. I worked in a bank. I was in charge of the card files. My desk was in the vault. I missed not having windows, but if there ever was a nuclear war, they said I would be one of the lucky ones.

WALTER. Job benefits are as important as salary.

JANE. Absolutely. Anyway, it wasn't a very demanding job. I could go for months without having to deal with anyone and it afforded me a great opportunity for my poetic pursuits.

WALTER. You read poetry?

JANE. I write poetry. My best one I called "Time."

WALTER. I'd love to hear it.

JANE. *(Flattered)* And so you shall, Walter Cranston.

(She stands to recite)

Time. By Jane Smite.

WALTER. A most beautiful and revealing name.

JANE. Thank you.

(Reciting)

Time. By Jane Smite.
TICK TOCK.
TOCK TICK.

(She sits)

WALTER. *(After a beat)* That's it?

JANE. They're very short. That's why I was able to write over thirty thousand of them.

WALTER. How prolific.

JANE. It kept me out of trouble.

(She stands again to recite)

Lonely. By Jane Smite.
EMPTY, EMPTY.
MY YESTERDAYS, MY TOMORROWS.

WALTER. *(Takes her hands and looks at her tenderly)* I share your pain, Jane Smite.

JANE. I knew that the minute I saw you, Walter Cranston.

WALTER. *(He kisses her)* I'm a Republican.

JANE. Why did you tell me that now?

WALTER. I just didn't want you to expect too much. Boy, this is working out so well for us. My not being satisfied with my life, you not being satisfied with yours, and now here we are together, so right for each other. I tell you, death is the greatest thing that ever happened to me. It really is.

JANE. Yes, yes. I feel that too, Walter.

(A woman ENTERS the bus station from street. She has curlers in her hair and wears a coat over her housecoat. It is **LORRAINE***, Walter's wife. She is carrying a briefcase)*

LORRAINE. Walter! Walter, you stupid imbecile, you forgot your sample case. I had to get dressed, leave my favorite soap and rush over here with it. Can't you ever go one day without screwing up? You are so damn inept.

(Shoves the briefcase into his gut)

Here, you dimwit.

WALTER. *(Taking case)* Thank you dear. That was sweet of you. Oh, uh…

(Introducing **JANE** *to* **LORRAINE***)*

Jane, this is my wife, Lorraine. Lorraine, this is Jane. Jane's a poet among other things. She and I were having this profound conversation about life and death.

JANE. It was quite wonderful. Some of it was very uplifting.

LORRAINE. Really? I'm thrilled for both of you. Let me know when you get back home, Walter. Sometimes days go by before I notice.

(She EXITS to street)

WALTER. *(Calling after her)* Thanks for bringing my briefcase, dear.

JANE. She seems very nice.

WALTER. Yes. She's a dandy little homemaker.

JANE. I guess then you were wrong. We aren't dead.

WALTER. No, I guess we aren't. Too bad. I was really hoping.

JANE. Oh, that's all right. It's a natural mistake. It's the times. We're all under such pressures.

WALTER. You're extremely understanding.

JANE. Thank you. But so disappointed. So very disappointed. *(She sits)*

HOWARD. *(Returning from phone)* I knew you two were loony. I just talked to my family. We are alive and I'm going to Toledo. How could I fall for something like that? They thought I was crazy.

STATION MASTER (V.O.) Attention! Attention! Bus for Toledo now boarding at Gate Number Four.

HOWARD. That's it, that's my bus. I hope it's not yours.

WALTER. I'm...I'm afraid it is.

HOWARD. The hell with it. I'll rent a car and *drive* to Toledo.

(He EXITS to street)

WALTER. I'm so sorry about all this. Raising your hopes about not being alive.

JANE. That's perfectly okay.

WALTER. I guess these things happen.

JANE. I know.

WALTER. God, I wish I were dead.

JANE. Don't say that. We'll get by. People like us do.

WALTER. At least we'll still have the bus ride, that is if you're going to Toledo.

JANE. No, I'm not taking the bus, Walter. I never do. I just come here from time to time and look at the people.

You find some fascinating people at a bus station, Walter, and you can make up marvelous things in your head about what their lives are like, and it doesn't matter whether you're right or wrong, because you've created these wonderful, wonderful stories about them that stay with you and if you're a romantic, as I am, they become very, very dear to you.

WALTER. But you didn't just see me today, you met me. We talked. We know about one another. You won't have to make anything up about me?

JANE. No, no, I won't. That's why you'll always be special. I really know you, don't I?

WALTER. Wouldn't it be just great if we both got on that bus and never came back?

JANE. Yes, it would. But that would be poetry and this is life, Walter. And we both know that life very seldom works out that agreeably.

WALTER. Yes, I imagine you're right.

JANE. You'd better buy your ticket.

WALTER. I can buy it on the bus. It's not crowded.

JANE. Most of my poems are love poems.

WALTER. Somehow I guessed that.

JANE. *(She rises)* Love Is Like A Bus. By Jane Smite. SOME PEOPLE SEEM TO BE WAITING FOR IT FOREVER. *(She sits)*

I wrote that one here. It's one of my longer ones.

WALTER. I'll never forget it.

JANE. You would have liked my other poems, Walter. All thirty thousand of them.

WALTER. Yes. I would have.

STATION MASTER (V.O.) Last call for Toledo. Bus departing Gate Number Four.

JANE. Goodbye, Walter.

WALTER. Goodbye, Jane.

(There is an awkward moment. Not knowing what to do, **WALTER** *shakes her hand and EXITS to bus.* **JANE**

stands, looks toward the doors that **WALTER** *left through for a moment and then faces the audience)*

JANE. *(Reciting)* Plays. By Jane Smite.
SOME HAVE HAPPY ENDINGS.
SOME DON'T.

(She sighs and EXITS to street, just as **FRANK** *and* **CLARA**, *a couple in their late twenties ENTER the Bus Station from street.* **CLARA** *seems calm,* **FRANK**, *apprehensive)*

CLARA. Nervous?

FRANK. Very.

CLARA. Don't be. It'll go fine.

FRANK. I just wish I was as sure as you.

CLARA. Frank, if you don't trust me after six years of marriage, then something's gone wrong. Now, you want to try it again?

FRANK. Here?

CLARA. There's no one around. The more you practice, the easier it will be.

FRANK. Maybe you're right.

CLARA. Of course, I am.

FRANK. I have to get my concentration together.

CLARA. *(Soothingly)* Just take your time.

FRANK. Okay. Okay. I think I got it.

(Pulls out a gun)

All right, this is a stick-up. Pull the bus over to the side of the road. How was that?

CLARA. Almost perfect.

FRANK. *(Panicked)* What did I miss? Tell me quick, Clara! What did I miss?

CLARA. One wrong move and I'll blow your fuckin' brains out.

FRANK. That's right. I forgot that part. That's very important, isn't it?

CLARA. It lends a certain authority.

FRANK. My God, what if he faints? What if the bus driver sees the gun and faints? What if he loses control of the bus and it goes off the road, hits a tree and explodes?

CLARA. Frank, we are living in the 21st century. The human animal has evolved to his highest magnitude. If a bus driver can't react responsibly to a simple holdup, he's got no right being in the transportation business.

FRANK. You're really good for me, Clara. You put everything in its proper perspective.

CLARA. We need this, Frank. We need this badly. You have failed at everything else in life. If you fail at armed robbery, what's left?

FRANK. I'll make good this time. I know I will.

(He puts the gun away)

CLARA. You failed as a bartender. You failed as a gas station attendant. You failed as a magazine salesman. You failed as an accountant…

FRANK. You can't count accounting. I was never trained for accounting. That was just a stab in the dark.

CLARA. And your last job, Frank. Remember how thrilled and hopeful we both were? I was sure you finally hit it.

FRANK. I wanted that one to work out more than anything in my life, Clara, so help me God. It was everything I ever wanted. I could have been content forever.

CLARA. A movie theatre attendant, Frank. You couldn't even make it as a movie theatre attendant.

FRANK. I loved that job. I got to tear up tickets and handle refreshments and sweep the carpet. God, I didn't want to lose that one. No one loved show business more than me.

CLARA. Remember how excited you were the day you learned they were giving you additional responsibilities?

FRANK. Yeah. Cleaning the bathrooms. I was really moving up in the company.

CLARA. Even our sex life went right that night.

FRANK. They shouldn't have fired me. I was the most dedicated employee they had.

CLARA. I don't care how dedicated you were, Frank. It was a stupid thing to wax the toilet seats. When I think of that poor skinny woman folded up in half and trapped for hours in that little bowl of water…

FRANK. To err is human.

CLARA. It cost the company three million dollars to settle the lawsuit.

FRANK. God, she was lucky. Becoming rich overnight just from using a strange bathroom. I tell you, Clara, it's all a matter of being in the right place at the right time. I never was.

CLARA. Maybe today you will be, Frank. Maybe today the wheel of fortune will land on your number. Maybe you were cut out to be anti-social all along .

FRANK. Oh, I hope so, Clara.

CLARA. I know you do, Frank. Now let's back away from hope and deal with the nitty-gritty face of reality. Shall we try it again?

FRANK. From the top?

CLARA. If you please and with sincerity. Make me proud of you, Frank, that's all I ask.

FRANK. I'll try. I really will.

(Clears throat)

This is a stick-up! Pull the bus over to the side of the road. One wrong move and I'll blow your fuckin' brains out!

CLARA. Almost! Almost!

FRANK. *(Upset)* What? What did I forget?

CLARA. The gun, Frank. If you don't pull out the gun, the bus driver will kick you in the balls and that will be that.

FRANK. *(Pulls out gun)* I hate this gun. I have no confidence in this gun. Why couldn't we get a real gun? Why do I have to use a toy?

CLARA. Because I don't believe in real guns, Frank. I happen to champion crime without violence.

FRANK. What if the bus driver is carrying a real gun? Did you ever consider that?

CLARA. Well, that's his tough luck. If he kills you, he'll have to live with it for the rest of his life. That's not a pretty future for him either, is it?

FRANK. I'm crap, Clara! I'm absolute crap!

CLARA. Please, Frank, up until now we were pursuing the collapse of your life with taste and dignity.

FRANK. I have no luck. I have no luck at all.

CLARA. Frank, you're starting to sound like a broken record.

FRANK. I'm a broken man.

CLARA. I refuse to believe that.

FRANK. I'm a failure, a nothing, a zero.

CLARA. You're the man I love.

FRANK. You deserved more, Clara.

CLARA. I know. I know.

FRANK. What do you mean, you know?

CLARA. I'm trying to calm you down, Frank. Now, let's go over the escape.

FRANK. This is the only part I like.

CLARA. After the holdup…

FRANK. I take the driver's keys and jump off the bus.

CLARA. Good. Then?

FRANK. I remove my ski mask and wait for you to pick me up.

CLARA. Perfect.

FRANK. Not perfect. I forgot the ski mask. I'm a loser, Clara. A loser!

CLARA. Where's the ski mask, Frank?

FRANK. At home in the bathroom.

CLARA. And what's it doing in the bathroom?

FRANK. It's drying. I wore it this morning when I took my shower. I was trying to get used to it.

CLARA. All right, Frank. Don't panic. Nothing's changed. Lucky for us you have a nondescript face.

FRANK. I'm not going through with it.

CLARA. You have to.

FRANK. Not without a mask.

CLARA. Frank, our backs are up against the wall. It's now a matter of putting food on the table.

FRANK. I'm not a criminal, Clara.

CLARA. Of course not. Not yet. But in an hour or two it will be a different story.

FRANK. It isn't fair. All I wanted out of life was to get through it as simply and as nicely as possible. No ax to grind, no grudge to bear. A nice, sincere person doing his best to make it through a world he doesn't quite understand or fit into.

CLARA. A sweet man.

FRANK. Yes.

CLARA. A kind man.

FRANK. Yes.

CLARA. An innocent man.

FRANK. Yes.

CLARA. I'm sorry, Frank, but I have no respect for that kind of person.

FRANK. I didn't think so.

CLARA. Unfortunately, we live in a time when power and success and how you come by it, is not as important as the fact that you have it. Common decency, love thy fellow man, those are all archaic expressions now. Stale, dated, useless. I hate to sound negative, Frank, but show me an honest man and I'll show you someone living below the poverty line.

FRANK. I just wonder if it's too late for me to change. I'm very set in my ways. I'm pushing thirty.

CLARA. Live by the gun, Frank. It's your only way out. Just think. No more begging. No more scraping and bowing. No more kissing anybody's ass. You'll finally

have a sense of importance. You'll be somebody at last.
FRANK. *(A beat)* You're good for me, Clara. You make everything so clear.
CLARA. I'm just being a supportive wife, Frank.
FRANK. You're right. What's the sense of going through life being a nobody even if it does make you happy. Honor, pride, love of country, values…for what? Bucks and bullshit, that's what it's all about. That's what America's come down to, hasn't it?
CLARA. It's frightening, Frank, but so it is written.
STATION MASTER (V.O.) Attention! Attention! The Number Six Bus for Saint Louis is now arriving from Indianapolis at Gate Number Two.
CLARA. That's your bus, Frank.
FRANK. I'll do it, Clara. If a life of crime is what I must pursue to have any decent self-image at all, then that's the road I'll take. But I'm not going to be just an ordinary criminal, Clara.
CLARA. No?
FRANK. The days of being ordinary are over for Frank Jones. From now on, I'll be the best, the most daring, the most fearless mastermind of evil this country has ever seen. Tales will be told of me. Novels will be written about me. My name will be legend in the realm of villainy.
CLARA. Now that's my man talking.
FRANK. My picture will be on every post office wall, my infamous name on every cop's lip.
CLARA. Lips! That's plural.
FRANK. Lips! Soon they'll give me a nickname like Baby Feet Frank. And you'll be at my side, Clara, as we go from city to city, state to state, taking what we want, when we want. Banks, jewelry stores, armored trucks, every once in a while a Starbucks. And it all started right here, with a simple little robbery on a bus headed

for St. Louis. So long, Doll. From this day on I'm a winner, you hear me? A winner! You'll have everything you want from now on, Clara, fancy clothes and fancy restaurants, and laughter, and wine, and above all a husband you can be proud of.

*(Suddenly a **BUS DRIVER** BURSTS through a door from the bus area)*

BUS DRIVER. The bus has been robbed! The bus has been robbed! Call the police! The bus has been robbed!

*(**FRANK** jumps in front of him to stop him)*

FRANK. What did they get?

BUS DRIVER. Everything.

FRANK. Everything?

BUS DRIVER. Everything!

(He continues towards the door to the street)

The bus has been robbed! Help! Police! The bus has been robbed!

*(The **BUS DRIVER** EXITS to street. **FRANK** sits on the bench, dejected)*

FRANK. I'm a loser, Clara. A loser.

*(**CLARA** goes to him and tenderly puts her hand in his)*

CLARA. I know, Frank. Still, it's nice to have dreams, isn't it?

*(They look at each other for a beat. **FRANK** rises and the two EXIT to street holding hands as a **BAG LADY** ENTERS from street carrying two overflowing shopping bags. She wears a ragged old coat, an old hat over her unkempt hair, her socks sag. She spots a newspaper and several magazines on the bench, immediately gathers them up and stuffs them in one of the bags. **FRED HAMPTON**, a conservatively dressed man, carrying a small suitcase and with a newspaper under his arm, ENTERS from the bus area. He looks at his watch, then goes to the bench to sit and wait when he notices the **BAG LADY** who has removed the lid of a trash can and is surveying the*

contents. He observes her curiously for a beat.)

BAG LADY. *(To* **FRED***)* Will you look at the trash some people throw away these days. There's some wonderful stuff here.

FRED. *(Finally recognizing her)* Maureen! Maureen Campbell!

BAG LADY. *(She looks closely at him and then in recognition smiles widely)* Freddy! Freddy Hampton! I can't believe it.

FRED. *(Delighted to see her)* Oh, my god, Maureen. How have you been? You look wonderful!

BAG LADY. Thanks. I feel good.

FRED. I can't get over it. How long's it been? Twenty-five, thirty years since we've seen each other? I swear, you haven't changed a bit.

BAG LADY. *(Proudly)* I jog.

FRED. It shows. You may not believe this, but so help me it's the truth. I was looking out the window of the bus and I have no idea why, but I thought to myself, I wonder what good old Maureen Campbell is doing now?

BAG LADY. No?

FRED. Can you believe the coincidence?

BAG LADY. Eerie, isn't it? Are you through with your paper?

FRED. *(Hands it to her)* Oh, sure, here.

BAG LADY. *(Takes it)* Thank you.

FRED. I did the crossword puzzle already.

BAG LADY. As long as the horoscope's still there. I don't make a move without checking my horoscope first. I swear, if not for astrology, I wouldn't be where I am today.

FRED. Yes, there must be something to it. Do you have time to talk? I don't want to keep you from anything urgent.

BAG LADY. No, no. All I have left is the train station and City Hall and I'm finished for the day.

FRED. So what's new? Ever see any of the old gang?

BAG LADY. Now and then. I saw Larry Petersen a couple of times at the city dump.

FRED. I knew he'd end up a bum.

BAG LADY. Not really. He owns a fleet of garbage trucks now. Has about forty employees.

FRED. Who would have guessed? I thought all he'd do is spend his whole life chasing girls.

BAG LADY. He still does. He even tried to come on to me once.

FRED. God bless him.

BAG LADY. That's what I said. And Bunny Tate, I ran into her.

FRED. Bunny, the home town beauty queen?

BAG LADY. She works at the Aluminum Can Redemption Center. I always try to get her window. She was never good at math so I usually end up with a better deal. Anyway, you won't believe it. She's as big as a house.

FRED. Oh, no! Sexy little Bunny. How could she let herself go like that?

BAG LADY. It's sad what some people do to themselves. She even got shorter.

FRED. I guess it could happen to anyone.

BAG LADY. That's exactly what I told her. And oh, Bradley Booker…

FRED. You saw old Brad?

BAG LADY. I was working the alley in back of his office and ran into him. He's a heart surgeon now and completely bald.

FRED. Brad bald? How do you like that? I used to envy his hair. It was so thick and curly.

BAG LADY. At times Mother Nature can really be cruel. Boy, I am so glad I never married him.

FRED. That's right. You two were an item.

BAG LADY. Just our sophomore year. He was too weird for me. All he wanted to do was talk about parts of the body. Mostly the insides.

FRED. I remember that. No one would sit with him at lunch.

(Pulls out a pack of cigarettes)

Mind if I have a cigarette? It's my last or I'd offer you one.

BAG LADY. That's okay. I don't smoke, but I'll take the empty package.

FRED. By all means.

(He hands her the package)

BAG LADY. Thanks.

(She folds it neatly and puts it in one of her bags)

FRED. *(Searching for a match)* Damn, I'm out of matches.

BAG LADY. Here, allow me.

(She takes a handful of cigarette lighters out of her pocket and holds them out to him)

Take your pick. I'll bet I have over eight hundred cigarette lighters. Some of them actually work.

FRED. Thanks.

(Lights lighter)

This one's fine.

(Lights his cigarette and hands her back the lighter)

BAG LADY. *(Putting the lighters back in her pocket)* You should really try to quit.

FRED. I know. I know.

BAG LADY. It's really a socially disgusting habit. People blowing their smelly breath all over you. I'm glad there's a three hundred dollar fine for smoking in public places.

FRED. You're right. I forgot. Thanks for reminding me.

(Throws the cigarette on the floor and steps on it)

BAG LADY. Good for you. By putting that out you just added three more minutes to your life.

FRED. Really?

BAG LADY. Yeah, I read all the health magazines. I'm really into health. I do yoga three times a week. I can put both my legs over my head.

(She takes a small tin container from her pocket, picks up the butt, puts it in the container and then puts the container in one of her bags)

This isn't for me. I have a friend who gives me four safety pins for every butt I give him.

FRED. I hope I didn't squash it too much.

BAG LADY. No, it's fine, fine. So what about you, Fred? You married, you have children?

FRED. Yes, in fact my wife should be here to pick me up any minute. We have two boys. One's the Mayor of Cleveland and the other is serving time in the state pen for embezzling.

BAG LADY. Oh, my. Isn't it something how two kids can grow up in the same house and be different as day and night. Remember my sister, Wanda?

FRED. Oh, yeah, sure. She was a couple years younger than us.

BAG LADY. We had all kinds of trouble with her. Drank, ran around, dropped out of school…We never thought she'd ever amount to anything.

FRED. And today?

BAG LADY. Actually she's doing remarkably well. She's living in Milwaukee, Wisconsin and has fourteen shopping carts.

FRED. I love to hear stories like that.

BAG LADY. You just gotta let kids be who they are. Eventually they all find themselves.

FRED. I hope so. How about some coffee?

BAG LADY. No, thanks, but I'll take the paper cup when you're finished.

*(**FRED** puts a coin in the machine. The empty cup comes down but no coffee. He pounds at the machine)*

FRED. I think the machine is broken. Nothing's coming out. You can't count on anything nowadays. Oh, well, here's the cup.

BAG LADY. Thanks.

(She takes the cup and puts it in one of her bags)

FRED. Listen, before I forget. I want your number. We've got to have dinner one night. Do you like sushi?

BAG LADY. Next to Mexican food it's my favorite.

FRED. Great. I'll give you a call next week and we'll set it up.

BAG LADY. Fine. I'll give you my number.

*(**FRED** takes out a pad and pen. The **BAG LADY** goes to the public phone)*

BAG LADY *(Continued)* It's 971-7771

FRED. *(Repeating)* 971-7771…Damn it, the pen's out of ink.

BAG LADY. I'll take it.

(She takes the pen and puts it in one of her bags)

FRED. Well, I've got most of it.

(Puts his note pad away)

You know something, Maureen, the years fly by so fast. I've been to a lot of places, seen a lot of things, but those early years we spent together, those were really the good old days, weren't they? I know it's wrong to live in the past, but I think of those times often. You want to see something?

(He opens his suitcase and takes out a high school sweater)

Look!

BAG LADY. Your high school sweater.

FRED. I take it everywhere. Once in a while when I feel kind of blue, I put it on and it cheers me right up. It makes me remember that part of my life when we didn't have to figure things out. We lived for the moment and who's to say that's not the way it's supposed to be.

(He removes his jacket and puts on the sweater)

BAG LADY. Keep it simple, keep it light. That's always been my theme.

FRED. Why is it we lose track of that?

(Modeling sweater)

How's this? Still fits.

BAG LADY. I adore the preppie look. *(Teasing)* Now, are you ready for something?

FRED. Go ahead.

*(The **BAG LADY** opens her coat revealing that she is wearing her high school sweater)*

BAG LADY. Taa Daa!

FRED. I don't believe it. You kept your high school sweater too.

BAG LADY. Uh huh. And underneath is my college one.

(Removing her coat)

Shall we?

FRED. You bet.

BAG LADY. You haven't forgotten?

FRED. Never.

(The two go into a cheer)

BOTH.
CENTRAL! CENTRAL! CENTRAL HIGH!
WE ARE HERE TO TOUCH THE SKY,
CENTRAL RAH! CENTRAL RAH!
WE ARE NUMBER ONE, HA HA

(They jump up, flinging their arms in the air)

Yeaaaaay Central!

FRED. I wonder if they still use the same cheer.

BAG LADY. I don't think so. They tore the school down last year.

FRED. I didn't know.

BAG LADY. You've got to read the papers.

(Indicates shopping bags)

I read all the papers. I've got them from 1981 on.

(SOUND: A car horn)

FRED. Oh, oh. That's probably Louise.

(He changes back into his jacket)

BAG LADY. Louise? Not Louise Hoffer?

FRED. Yes, you remember her? She was that cute brunette with the pug nose.

BAG LADY. Oh, sure. She used to sleep with the entire football team.

FRED. Yes, she's a good-time girl. That's what I liked best about her.

BAG LADY. Well, give her my love.

FRED. *(Putting sweater in suitcase)* I will, Maureen. And you take care.

(He starts to close his suitcase but as an after thought takes out several folded plastic laundry bags)

Hey, maybe you might want these? They're laundry bags from my hotel.

BAG LADY. *(Taking them)* Oh, they're beautiful. Thank you. I don't see many of these around. At least not clean ones.

FRED. As a rule I leave them in the room, but today I had a feeling.

(Closes his suitcase and extends his hand to her)

It's really been nice seeing you, Maureen. You sure made my day.

BAG LADY. And you made mine, Fred.

FRED. Bye!

BAG LADY. Bye bye.

*(**FRED** EXITS to street)*

BAG LADY *(Continued) (A beat)*
CENTRAL! CENTRAL! CENTRAL HIGH!

(She nods her head sadly and puts on her coat over her sweater)

Oh, well, we all have to grow up sometime.

(She takes her two shopping bags and EXITS to street

as **AUDREY**, *a young woman, ENTERS from street, looks around, takes a whisk broom from her handbag, sweeps off a spot in the middle of the floor and lies down.* **ERNEST**, *a somewhat older businessman carrying a briefcase and a newspaper, ENTERS from street. He looks at his watch, then crosses to the bench where* **AUDREY** *is lying, sees her, stops, looks at her for a moment and then he puts his briefcase down, sits, unfolds his paper, looks over at* **AUDREY** *once more, and then begins reading)*

AUDREY. *(A beat. Not moving)* Aren't you even curious?

ERNEST. *(Behind his paper)* Nope.

AUDREY. I find that hard to believe.

ERNEST. Don't.

AUDREY. I do. I find it very hard to believe and extremely callous.

ERNEST. It's been a long day. I'm on my way home. Everything went well. I'm a very private person. I'm not in the mood for a significant encounter.

AUDREY. I could be dying, you know. I could have had a massive stroke.

ERNEST. *(Putting aside newspaper)* I looked at your color. It looked good. You seemed to be breathing normally and one of your eyes was open. I say let well enough alone.

AUDREY. *(Rising)* People like you make me sick. People without concern for anyone but themselves.

ERNEST. My dear woman, I have been informed many times by those who know me, that familiarity breeds contempt.

AUDREY. I was not asking for familiarity. I was asking for a simple, helping hand. Was that so difficult? You let me lay here like a diseased animal. A possible victim of a brutal attack. You could have at least called the fire department or the paramedics, but no. You'd rather look the other way, wouldn't you, you dirty son of a bitch!

ERNEST. I am going to remain a gentleman and not demand an apology for such pissy language.

AUDREY. It was much easier for you to ignore my dire condition. There would have been questions, red tape, papers to fill out, and frankly, it did not make good sense to you to go through all that for a perfect stranger. Admit it, you uncaring bastard! Admit it!

ERNEST. Will you leave me alone then?

AUDREY. Who'd want any part of you, you low life jerk!

ERNEST. Okay, I admit it. I did not choose to get caught up in a dubious situation with someone I didn't know and don't care to know, now more than ever. So help me God.

(**MARSHA**, *an older woman, ENTERS the bus station from street*)

AUDREY. *(Militantly)* I want your name.

ERNEST. Please, you said you'd leave me alone.

AUDREY. I want your name!

ERNEST. I'm not giving it to you.`

AUDREY. *(She hits him with her bag)* No good dirty rotten pig!

ERNEST. Hey, stop it!

MARSHA. What's going on here? I sense trouble?

AUDREY. *(Indicates* **MARSHA***)* See! An innocent bystander who's not afraid to get involved.

MARSHA. Of course not.

AUDREY. I was lying on the floor, right down there, possibly unconscious, possibly deathly ill, possibly even a victim of a drive by shooting and *he* totally ignored me.

MARSHA. Is that right?

ERNEST. I don't want to discuss it.

MARSHA. *(Slaps him on the shoulders)* Swine!

ERNEST. Oooow! That hurt.

MARSHA. Vermin like you don't belong in a civilized society.

AUDREY. Tell him!

ERNEST. *(Rubbing his shoulder)* She hit me!

MARSHA. Did you get his name?

AUDREY. He wouldn't give it to me.

ERNEST. *(Indicating the far end of the room)* Look, I'm just going to sit quietly over there and continue reading my paper and pretend it's tomorrow and I'm somewhere else.

(He puts the newspaper under his arm, rises and picks up his briefcase)

MARSHA. Crummy low life!

*(As **ERNEST** attempts to walk away, **MARSHA** grabs his free arm and twists it behind his back. **ERNEST** continues to hold his briefcase with the other hand)*

ERNEST. Oowwwwww!

MARSHA. Get his wallet.

ERNEST. You're hurting me.

(Audrey quickly goes through Ernest's jacket pockets and removes his wallet from his inside pocket)

AUDREY. I've got it. He had it hidden in his jacket pocket.

ERNEST. Oh, a robbery. Thank goodness. I'm relieved. For a moment I thought you were a couple of every day psychopaths.

AUDREY. *(Looking in his wallet)* Here's his social security card. Ernest Running Bear. How do you like that? A foreigner. You would think a foreigner might appreciate the values of this country a little bit more than most. Snake!

(She hits him with her handbag again)

ERNEST. Look, I won't even wait for the bus, okay? I'll take a cab home. It's only a hundred and ten miles.

*(He yanks his wallet from **AUDREY** and crams it in his pocket)*

MARSHA. Sure, leave. Leave the scene of your infamous inaction. You know what I want to do? I want to hit you again.

ERNEST. Please, don't.

MARSHA. *(To **AUDREY**)* Here, you hold him.

AUDREY. Right.

(**AUDREY** *takes possession of* **ERNEST**'s *twisted arm*)

ERNEST. Now, wait…

(**MARSHA** *punches* **ERNEST** *in the stomach*)

ERNEST *(Continued)* Ooooofff! You're nuts! You're both nuts! Help! Help me, someone!

(**AL**, *a cop, ENTERS from street*)

AL. All right! What's going on here?

ERNEST. Oh, officer, thank goodness you're here. I was just waiting for the bus when…

(*Indicates* **AUDREY**)

… this insane woman…

AL. You mean my wife?

ERNEST. Your wife? That's your wife?

AL. Hello, Audrey.

(*Kisses her*)

I love you so much.

ERNEST. Okay. Okay, forget her.

(*Indicates* **MARSHA**)

This is the real maniac. I never dealt with such violence. Twisting my arm off, punching me in the stomach… This one should not be allowed on the streets.

AL. You mean my mother?

ERNEST. Your mother? This woman's your mother?

MARSHA. Hello, son.

(*They kiss*)

AL. Hello, mom.

ERNEST. *(Trying to get away)* Excuse me. I think I'm going to lay down in front of a bus.

AL. No, you don't.

(*The women hold him.* **AL** *walks around* **ERNEST** *in military fashion, slapping his night stick into the palm of his hand*)

AL. *(Continued)* So, another one who considers himself a human being and yet refuses to come to the aid of his fellow man. That's not a very gracious attitude, is it?

AUDREY. Scumbag!

MARSHA. Dick head!

STATION MASTER (V.O.) Attention! Attention! Bus Number Seven now loading at Gate Number Two.

ERNEST. That's my bus! Look, all I want to do is get on it and get the hell out of here. Let's forget this whole thing and I'll never come back to this town again. I promise.

AL. Sure, who wouldn't like to get off that easy? Fortunately there are some of us who refuse to live in your kind of world.

ERNEST. I live in a wonderful world. I don't talk to my neighbors and they don't talk to me. It's perfect.

AL. Fortunately, there are some of us who know if one hurts, we all hurt. If one bleeds, we all bleed. If one is persecuted, we all are persecuted.

ERNEST. I think right now I come under all three categories.

AUDREY. Hurt him, Al. I want him to suffer the way he would have left me to suffer.

(The women release **ERNEST**. **AL** *circles him, jabbing him with his night stick)*

AL. I can't believe what a worm you are not to even care about my wife. This sweet, little, innocent, fine, sexy woman, lying on the ground in agony...

ERNEST. I do care, I do, Officer. But there was nothing wrong with her. I swear.

AL. *(Continuing to jab him)* Indifferent, repulsive affront to mankind.

ERNEST. Ooooowww!

MARSHA. How do you like a taste of your own medicine, huh, big shot? Now who's going to help you?

*(***AL** *pushes* **ERNEST** *towards* **MARSHA** *who knees him in the groin)*

ERNEST. Oooooohhh!

(ERNEST *reels from the impact and ends up facing* AUDREY *who is about to hit him with her handbag again*)

AUDREY. Unemotional piece of sewage.

ERNEST. *(Throwing his hands in the air)* Wait! Wait! Stop! I see what you're doing. I see the point you're making.

MARSHA. Don't listen to him. He's probably just trying to save his neck, the weasel.

ERNEST. No, I swear. I get it! I really get it! I see where you're going with all this.

AUDREY. You'd better not be stalling.

AL. I'll break both his legs if he is.

ERNEST. It's so obvious, so simple, yet so true. The indifference that we show towards one another. It could be fatal to all of us.

MARSHA. Go on.

ERNEST. Suddenly, it's so beautifully clear to me. No man is an island. Do unto others as you would have them do unto you.

AUDREY. Did you hear that? Did I note a touch of unselfish regard?

MARSHA. Oh, my God. Have we actually lit one small candle?

ERNEST. Yes. Yes, that's it in a nutshell. One good turn deserves another. You scratch my back and I'll scratch yours and of course, to get, you've got to give.

AUDREY. I wish I had my tape recorder. This belongs in the *Readers Digest*.

ERNEST. Man must live in a world of cooperation and compassion or it's no world at all. It is a lethal blunder to emotionally cut ourselves off from one another.

AL. One is a lonely number.

ERNEST. From this moment on, I am no longer cold, dispassionate and withdrawn. I am no longer an unconcerned shell. I am a human being with feelings. I can give. I can nourish. I promise you all, I will never, ever be indifferent to my fellow man again. I will respond to him with all my heart. My fellow man is me. I am my fellow man. For the first time in my life I actually feel love for him. And I acquired that ability here. From you wonderful, wonderful, people. Thank you, thank you.

(He shakes everyone's hand)

Yes, yes, yes!

(He grabs his briefcase and runs to the doors leading to the bus)

It's a brand new me! A brand spanking new me!

(He EXITS. There is a beat as the others look on, impressed)

AL. Can you believe that?

MARSHA. I wouldn't have if I didn't see it with my own eyes, hear it with my own ears.

AUDREY. We actually took an unresponsive piece of slime and turned him completely around.

MARSHA. It just proves that people like us can definitely make a difference

*(**AL** puts his arm around his mother, **MARSHA**)*

AL. With just a little effort, a little common sense, a little adjustment of attitude, we taught that scuzz bucket to feel, to care, to be concerned.

AUDREY. We have already made this a better world.

MARSHA. A much better world.

AUDREY. Right. So, it's now back to work.

(Proudly out to audience with a smile)

One down. Six and a half billion more to go. We're well on our way.

(She spreads herself on the floor as...)

THE LIGHTS DIM TO BLACK

End of Act I

ACT II

AT RISE:

(**MRS. EVANS**, *a middle-aged woman, somberly dressed, waits silently on the bench.* **MR. WADE**, *about the same age, also somberly dressed and carrying a small package ENTERS from bus area, looks around, spots* **MRS. EVANS** *and goes to her.*)

MR. WADE. Mrs. Evans?

MRS. EVANS. *(Rising)* Mr. Wade.

MR. WADE. How do you do.

MRS. EVANS. How do you do.

MR. WADE. Mrs. Evans, I can't tell you how sorry we all are.

MRS. EVANS. I understand.

MR. WADE. The mortuary has never made a mistake like this before, never, and we're extremely grateful that you've decided not to take any legal recourse.

MRS. EVANS. I'm not that kind of a person, Mr. Wade.

MR. WADE. No. I can see you're not.

(Presents her with a box)

Well, here he is.

MRS. EVANS. *(Takes box and looks at it)* This is Harry?

MR. WADE. Maybe you'd better sit down.

MRS. EVANS. Maybe I'd better.

(They both sit)

MR. WADE. When we found out we cremated the wrong person, I can't tell you how embarrassing it was. I mean our faces were literally red.

MRS. EVANS. I'll bet.

MR. WADE. But you see, they both came in at the very same time, your husband and the clown. We should have at least checked their suits.

MRS. EVANS. I'm sure that would have made a difference.

MR. WADE. Well, like they say, hind sight is twenty-twenty. Now you still have the clown?

MRS. EVANS. Yes. He's in the baggage department.

MR. WADE. Ready to ship?

MRS. EVANS. Yes. I tried to arrange him as close to the way I remembered seeing him at the services.

MR. WADE. That was very thoughtful. It must have been a terrible shock for you and everyone walking into the chapel to discover the clown instead of your beloved husband.

MRS. EVANS. Well, at first it was, but slowly the crowd lightened up and actually there was a good deal of laughter. Perhaps you should have taken the clown's make-up off before you shipped him. At least his fake nose.

MR. WADE. You're absolutely right. I'm going to give that note at the next staff meeting.

MRS. EVANS. Of course a lot of Harry's friends went with the situation. They thought I was making a statement.

MR. WADE. Really?

MRS. EVANS. Yes. Possibly, that death and comedy go hand in hand.

MR. WADE. Interesting.

MRS. EVANS. Even the Minister was affected. He threw away his sermon and started telling jokes.

MR. WADE. I'm sure it must have seemed like the right thing to do.

MRS. EVANS. Frankly, I thought some of his humor was a bit too ethnic. Several of our Chinese friends walked out.

MR. WADE. Oh, that's too bad.

MRS. EVANS. Not really. They missed the bomb scare. A terrorist mistook the building we were in for a government office.

MR. WADE. Oh, yes. I remember. That was on the six o'clock news. Was that at your husband's funeral?

MRS. EVANS. *(Correcting him)* Service. There was no funeral.

MR. WADE. Yes. Of course.

MRS. EVANS. I didn't think it was right for me to bury the clown especially since the grave site was right next to

Harry's mother, who I'm sorry to say, died without any sense of humor at all.

MR. WADE. Well, I promise you, Mrs. Evans, we will do our best to make this all up to you.

MRS. EVANS. That's all right. I can only believe that something good comes out of everything. By the way, Mr. Wade, how did he die?

MR. WADE. The clown or your husband?

MRS. EVANS. Why don't you take them in alphabetical order.

MR. WADE. Well, the clown was killed when the midget shot him out of the cannon.

MRS. EVANS. How tragic.

MR. WADE. It really wasn't the midget's fault. He was distracted by the Fat Lady.

MRS. EVANS. Why? What did she do?

MR. WADE. She fell off the high wire. You see it created such a ruckus the midget forgot to aim the cannon and instead of the net, the clown hit the lemonade stand.

MRS. EVANS. And the fat lady? She landed on…

MR. WADE. Your husband.

MRS. EVANS. Basically it's the luck of the draw isn't it.

MR. WADE. Death was instantaneous for all of them.

MRS. EVANS. Thank God for small favors.

MR. WADE. My feelings exactly.

MRS. EVANS. *(Looks at the package)* Poor Harry. Two weeks ago he left a strong, handsome one hundred and eighty pound man and now here he is back in town, a little twelve ounce package.

MR. WADE. It's a wild, wacky world, isn't it? Now, what about yourself, Mrs. Evans? What are your plans now that you're…widowed?

MRS. EVANS. Well, financially I'll be fine. There was a little insurance money and actually the Fat Lady falling on Harry was a stroke of luck because there was double indemnity for accidental death.

MR. WADE. How nice. And what about suing the circus? You could probably pick up a nice piece of change there.

MRS. EVANS. Oh, no, no. For all the joy the circus brought Harry, I know he wouldn't want me to do that.

MR. WADE. You're an extremely fair woman, Mrs. Evans.

MRS. EVANS. Yes, yes, I am. Harry always said I was. I think that's the reason our marriage was so successful. I never made any unnecessary demands on him, never criticized his work, always trusted him…In all modesty, I was a wonderful wife.

MR. WADE. Just meeting you for these few minutes authenticates that completely. Which reminds me. We found this in Harry's pocket. I believe this verifies his great love for you.

(He removes a small gift box from his pocket and hands it to **MRS. EVANS***)*

I think you'll appreciate this package a little more than the first one I presented you.

MRS. EVANS. *(She opens it up and produces a bracelet)* Oh, my. A bracelet.

MR. WADE. There's only a slight dent in it from the impact.

MRS. EVANS. *(About to break down)* My God, Harry. Why did you always have to have a front row seat?

MR. WADE. Please, Mrs. Evans, don't do that to yourself. You've been remarkably strong up until now.

MRS. EVANS. I'm sorry. He was such a fine man.

MR. WADE. It's inscribed, Mrs. Evans.

MRS. EVANS. What?

MR. WADE. The bracelet. Read it. It's inscribed on the inside.

MRS. EVANS. *(Reading)* "To my darling, Annie. I'll love you always. Harry."

MR. WADE. To the end he thought of you, his darling Annie.

MRS. EVANS. I'm Eleanor.

MR. WADE. What?

MRS. EVANS. I'm Eleanor. I don't even know an Annie.

MR. WADE. *(An awkward beat)* Uh, maybe it belonged to the clown.

MRS. EVANS. No. It was Harry's. I'm not going to lie to you about Harry's fidelity. Harry had lots of women. I knew that. I tried to ignore it. After all, he was a traveling salesman, on the road a lot, what could I expect?

MR. WADE. My God, Mrs. Evans. In my entire life I never met anyone as understanding and forgiving as you.

MRS. EVANS. But at home he belonged to me and that's what counts, doesn't it?

(She places bracelet back in box and then puts box in her purse)

MR. WADE. Your attitude, it's absolutely marvelous. You are one in a million, Mrs. Evans. One in a million.

MRS. EVANS. Thank you, Mr. Wade.

MR. WADE. Maybe Harry was unlucky at the circus, but it's obvious he was certainly lucky at home.

STATION MASTER (V.O.) Bus Number Six now boarding for South Bend.

MR. WADE. That's mine. I'm going to have to go. There are some people waiting for the clown.

MRS. EVANS. Oh, he had a family?

MR. WADE. He was living with the Elephant Woman.

MRS. EVANS. I'm so sorry.

MR. WADE. Don't be. I understand it was a tempestuous relationship at best. A lot of professional jealousy.

MRS. EVANS. Then this mishap could be a blessing in disguise.

MR. WADE. It seems to be the case. *(Rises)* Well, I'll be saying goodbye.

MRS. EVANS. *(Rises)* Oh, do I owe you anything for Harry?

MR. WADE. Don't be silly. It's on the house. Besides, we'll more than make up for it when we bill the circus for the Fat Lady. We plan to charge by the pound for her.

MRS. EVANS. I'm happy for you.

MR. WADE. *(Extends hand)* It was truly a pleasure meeting you, Mrs. Evans. You're a woman of great courage and understanding. I know your husband would be very proud of you if he could see you now.

MRS. EVANS. *(Takes his hand)* Well, then, let's hope he can. Goodbye, Mr. Wade.

*(**MR. WADE** EXITS to bus area. **MRS. EVANS** stands there for a beat, looking after him. She sighs and then walks to a trash can and address the package with Harry's ashes.)*

And goodbye to you too, Harry, you cheating son-of-a-bitch!

*(She drops the package into the trash can and EXITS to street as **BOBBY**, a young man in jeans, t-shirt and sneakers and **JUNE**, a young woman in a wedding dress ENTER from street. **BOBBY** goes to the ticket window and quickly purchases two tickets and then goes to **JUNE** who has been bouncing around excitedly)*

JUNE. I've never been happier or more excited in my entire life.

BOBBY. You mean it?

JUNE. Of course, I mean it. Oh, Bobby, it's so crazy.

BOBBY. I know. That's what makes it so wonderful, because it is so crazy.

JUNE. And so romantic. So absolutely romantic. I mean for you to show up at the church the way you did. Right before I was about to say "I do". Oh, wow. It was so dramatic and everything. I was literally speechless.

BOBBY. When I found out about you getting married, well, something inside me just snapped. I couldn't let you do it. I would have hated myself forever if I did.

JUNE. I'll bet. Oh, Bobby, all these years never hearing from you.

BOBBY. I know.

JUNE. I was sure you had forgotten all about me.

BOBBY. Never. Never for a minute. Never for a second.

JUNE. *(Looks at him)* I'll bet you really mean it.

BOBBY. I'm nuts about you, June. I've always been and now more than ever.

(He kisses her)

JUNE. Oh, God, it's so insane. So absolutely outrageous. To be carried off at the altar by an old boyfriend. Oh, Bobby, this is just the way I always hoped my wedding day would turn out. I swear I'll never forget this as long as I live. Never.

BOBBY. I don't think many people will. Especially your father. I've never seen anyone look so pale in my life. I hope he'll be okay.

JUNE. Oh, sure, he'll be fine. Ever since they put in that new pacemaker he's been able to deal with emotional stress better than ever. It's my mother I'm really concerned about. The months she spent planning the reception. I'm so sorry I encouraged a sit-down meal instead of a buffet. She might have been able to freeze a buffet. You know we were actually serving both soup and salad. You don't get that at many weddings. Plus an appetizer, plus a choice of chicken or fish for the main course.

BOBBY. I wouldn't blame her if she never talks to either of us again.

JUNE. And the music. Wasn't that something? Twelve violins and an oboe. Arnold paid for that, the flowers and the liquor. What a waste. It's almost a shame we didn't have the reception first. You never did tell me how you like my dress.

BOBBY. It's beautiful. You're beautiful.

JUNE. You know, Bobby, I was beginning to think this day was going to be a real dud. Especially after they lost the wedding cake.

BOBBY. They lost the wedding cake?

JUNE. Imagine, a wedding without a wedding cake. It could have ruined the whole thing. I'll bet you money Arnold is going to sue the pants off the caterer.

BOBBY. Even now?

JUNE. Oh, sure. Arnold is a lawyer. They have a need to get even just out of principle.

BOBBY. Look, forget Arnold, forget the wedding. From now on let's just think about us, okay?

JUNE. Oh, that's such a good idea.

BOBBY. Besides, time has a way of healing everything.

JUNE. Isn't that the truth? For instance, take you and me. Two people who throughout all these years apart never stopped caring about each other, thinking about each other.

BOBBY. Never.

JUNE. Well, I, for the life of me, can't remember why we broke up, can you?

BOBBY. You don't remember?

JUNE. No. All I recall is that we were going together for a while and then one day you stopped showing up.

BOBBY. I know. I guess I wasn't ready to settle down. I wanted to see the world. I wanted to know what life was all about.

JUNE. *(Expecting more)* Uh huh?

BOBBY. That's basically it.

JUNE. Oh. Well, I'm glad you came back because…because I swear nothing could have made me this happy. Not even the Cherries Jubilee. That's what we were having for dessert along with the lost cake. It was going to be a dynamite event.

BOBBY. You wouldn't have been happy married to a lawyer, June. I've met a few of them. They're all the same. No imagination. No scope. They live in a closed box and that's the way he would have forced you to live. A life of isolation. Buried between four walls.

JUNE. I couldn't live that way.

BOBBY. Who could?

JUNE. Not me.

BOBBY. What kind of law did he practice?

JUNE. International. He said we'd have to travel all over the world a lot.

BOBBY. He did? Well, believe me, you would have been very uncomfortable. They hate American lawyers.

JUNE. Where?

BOBBY. Everywhere.

JUNE. You're probably right. Plus all the packing and unpacking. Which reminds me. I guess Mom will have to give all the gifts back. His Aunt Hilda was giving us luggage. His folks gave us our silver and his firm gave us the niftiest gift ever, a fifty inch flat screen TV with over three hundred and fifty channels. I'd never run out of things to watch.

BOBBY. Uh, June...

JUNE. But who cares? I got the best wedding gift a bride could get. You! Forever and ever, till death do us part.

BOBBY. That's what I want to hear.

JUNE. Oh, Bobby, from now on, whither thou goest, I will go.

BOBBY. That's beautiful.

JUNE. It's from the Bible. I was going to say that to Arnold after the lobster bisque. But now I'll say it to you. Whither thou goest, I will go.

BOBBY. That's my girl.

JUNE. Whither goest thou, Bobby?

BOBBY. Huh?

JUNE. Where is it we're going? I mean I saw you buy bus tickets and I just wonder where we're going.

BOBBY. Cincinnati.

JUNE. *(Disappointed)* Oh, no.

BOBBY. We don't have to stay there. I just asked for tickets for the first bus out of here. We can go anywhere. There's nothing to tie us down. You and I are free to

go and do what we want to do the rest of our lives.
JUNE. You mean you have no definite plans?
BOBBY. *(Takes her hand)* I'm still a dreamer, June.
JUNE. No kidding?
BOBBY. Yes. And now I have you to dream with me.
JUNE. We were going to Acapulco.
BOBBY. Who?
JUNE. Arnold and me. For our honeymoon. He rented a suite on the ocean. We were going to spend three weeks there and then two weeks in Rio.
BOBBY. He was so shallow, wasn't he?
JUNE. On the surface he seemed that way.
BOBBY. There's so much more to life than material things. Look at me. Happy as a lark and I don't have a thing.
JUNE. No?
BOBBY. Nothing.
JUNE. Come on, Bobby, everybody's got something.
BOBBY. Like what?
JUNE. Like a job, like a profession, like a lawyer.
BOBBY. Life is my profession.
JUNE. No, kidding?
BOBBY. Money, possessions…what do they mean? All they do is cloud the real purpose of man. To enjoy the sunshine, the trees, the stars, the moon…
JUNE. That is so romantic.
BOBBY. One thing you're going to find out about me. I am not impressed by the mundane trappings of society.
JUNE. And neither am I…now. But I wonder what Arnold is going to do with the house?
BOBBY. What house?
JUNE. The one he bought for us. You should see it. A ten room Colonial right on the river.
BOBBY. Ten rooms! How ridiculous.
JUNE. I know. And with a guest house.

BOBBY. Obscene!

JUNE. I know. And with a tennis court and a pool.

BOBBY. Nothing but tawdry middle class flash!

JUNE. I know. Which reminds me, I'm still wearing his three and a half carat engagement ring.

(Showing it to BOBBY)

Legally, do I have to return it to him or not?

BOBBY. *(A bit annoyed)* I don't know. I don't care. Throw it in the garbage if you like.

JUNE. Oh, you're jealous. Don't be. No matter what Arnold could give me, it will never compare to what I have with you.

(Remembering)

Oh, my God, my Mercedes!

BOBBY. Your what?

JUNE. My Mercedes. Another thing Arnold gave me. It needs servicing and Arnold won't know where I put the keys.

BOBBY. He bought you a Mercedes, too?

JUNE. For Valentine's Day. You know, the small eighty thousand dollar convertible. I mean, he had to get me something.

BOBBY. *(Impatient)* Where the hell's that damn bus?

JUNE. I'm so excited. Here we are, together after all these years. It's just like a fairy tale, Bobby. Rescued by the handsome young Prince, to live happily ever after and then some.

BOBBY. I sure hope so.

(They look at each other for a beat)

JUNE. So what have you been doing with your life, Bobby?

BOBBY. *(A bit upset)* I told you. Whatever I wanted to do. I've traveled the country. From Ohio to Nebraska. From Tennessee to North Dakota.

JUNE. Sounds fabulous.

BOBBY. It was.

JUNE. What about Acapulco? Have you ever been to Acapulco?

BOBBY. No. Actually, I never left the states.

JUNE. Well, we just have to go some day. Arnold said the ocean is as blue as the water in the swimming pool in back of our Colonial house right next to the tennis court.

BOBBY. I hope it all burns down.

JUNE. Oh, Bobby, don't be like that. I would much rather live in a run-down shack with you than in any mansion with Arnold.

BOBBY. You really mean that?

JUNE. I certainly do. As long as there's a place for the baby.

BOBBY. *(Stunned)* The baby?

JUNE. I was waiting for the right time to tell you. I hope it won't spoil things, but I'm having Arnold's baby.

BOBBY. A baby?

JUNE. Fourth month. That's why I picked this wedding dress. Doesn't show a thing.

BOBBY. You...You're pregnant?

JUNE. God, I ordered so much baby furniture. I hope Arnold knows where to put it all, although he really won't need it now, will he?

BOBBY. A baby? You're having a baby?

JUNE. That's why I thought the Mercedes was so impractical. By the time you put in the play pen, the car seat and the diaper bag, there's no room for people.

BOBBY. You're having a baby!

JUNE. You know, Bobby, you must really love me to do a weird thing like this, running away with me. Especially now that you know I'm pregnant.

BOBBY. June, in all fairness, you just told me about it this minute.

JUNE. If it's a boy, maybe it's only right to call him Arnold. After you know who.

STATION MASTER (V.O.) Attention! Bus Number Three now boarding for Cincinnati.

JUNE. That's our bus, Bobby. Try to find a seat next to a window that opens. I have a tendency to throw up a lot lately.

BOBBY. June, June, look at me.

JUNE. Yes, Bobby.

BOBBY. It's a far, far better thing I'm going to do today than I have ever done in my life. June, I've decided to give you up.

JUNE. Again?

BOBBY. June, I have no job, no future.

JUNE. Arnold once said if he was starting all over he would definitely get into computer technology.

BOBBY. But that would mean an office, a desk, regular hours…

JUNE. With the baby screaming all day long, you'll be glad to get out of the house. Oh, I love you, Bobby. Hold me.

BOBBY. Listen to me, June! I think I made a big mistake coming here today. I mean, I love you madly, but there's more to life than love. There's also self preservation.

STATION MASTER (V.O.) Last call for Bus Number Three for Cincinnati.

BOBBY. That's my bus!

JUNE. *Your* bus?

BOBBY. I can't take you with me, June. I can't. There comes a time when we have to think about Arnold.

JUNE. Which one? Big Arnold or Little Arnold.

BOBBY. Every Arnold. Forget me, June. I wouldn't be good for you. I have a compulsion to live a very unstable life. Being a father at this point in my life is a total impossibility and just the thought of it is unthinkable.

JUNE. I'm confused. Could you please, repeat everything after, "Forget me, June"?

BOBBY. *(Hands her a ticket)* Here. Cash in this bus ticket and take a cab back to the church. Maybe it's not too late. Maybe all the gifts are still there. I'll try to send you a little something myself.

JUNE. But, Bobby...

BOBBY. Goodbye, June. Best of luck. Nice seeing you again.

(He EXITS thru doors to bus area)

JUNE. But, Bobby...

*(**BOBBY** is gone. **JUNE** takes a beat. She is relieved)*

Boy, did I almost screw up!

(She lifts her dress and removes a cell phone from her garter belt, dials and then speaks)

Mother! Are you still at the church? Arnold too? Good. Tell him to hang in. I'm grabbing a cab and I'll be right back. Oh, Mother, I have really grown up in the last fifteen minutes. I left that church a silly, foolish girl but I am coming back a sensible, mature woman. I'm going to make Arnold the best little wife I can and maybe in five or six years when I'm tired of watching TV, maybe I'll even have a baby.

*(She hangs up and EXITS to street as **MACE**, a bus driver in his fifties ENTERS from the bus area. He carries a thermos of coffee. He looks around for a few beats, shakes his head in disappointment, sighs, sits down, takes off his cap and pours himself a cup of coffee. **LAURA**, a bus company employee about the same age, ENTERS from behind the ticket booth with a sandwich)*

MACE. Hello, Laura.

LAURA. Hello, Mace. Mind if I join you?

MACE. I was hoping you would.

LAURA. *(Sits next to **MACE**)* I never ate out here before. Always had to eat behind that cage. But I guess the last day no one's gonna mind. Any passengers come in with you?

MACE. No. Any going out with me?

LAURA. No.

MACE. What a shame.

LAURA. Isn't it.

MACE. Wonder what they're gonna do with this old place? I hate to see them tear it down.

LAURA. Actually, I heard someone say it's either gonna be a church or a restaurant or maybe it was a combination church and restaurant. I really wasn't listening too closely. Whatever it'll be, it'll be, and without us.

MACE. Still, I'm gonna miss it. Been making this stop for almost thirty years.

LAURA. I know.

MACE. You're not upset?

LAURA. Says who? But I saw it coming. Today traveling's mostly about planes and cars. Bus business hasn't been good for a long time.

MACE. I know. I'm surprised they kept the company going for as long as they did.

LAURA. I had it all explained to me once. Something to do with government subsidy. As long they were losing money, between maintenance, depreciation, and a couple tax loopholes, they were actually making money. But then when this electronic company bought the bus company, they had to liquidate it immediately for the write-off in order to save their shirt factory down in Georgia which is gonna start making Japanese cars in two years.

MACE. The world belongs to accountants.

LAURA. Looks that way. I'm just not sure they deserve it.

MACE. *(Pouring some coffee from his thermos)* Coffee?

LAURA. Thanks. I'll get my cup.

(She goes for coffee mug)

How about half a sandwich?

MACE. Sure. I am kind of hungry. I ate my lunch at ten o'clock.

LAURA. What time did you start work?

MACE. Nine.

LAURA. I've had days like that. By two-thirty you've eaten all three meals and you've got nothing to look forward to for the rest of the day.

(Comes out with coffee mug)

I usually have some coffee made, but since today wasn't going to be a full day, I didn't bother.

(Mace pours her coffee)

What's in it?

MACE. Just a little sugar, a little cream.

LAURA. Perfect.

MACE. Yeah? Great. *(Sighs)* It's a hell of a time in our lives to have to start over, isn't it?

LAURA. Yeah, it is, but I guess you can always find something to do if you really want to. Frankly, with the pension and the severance pay, I'll be okay for awhile. What about you?

MACE. Oh, I'm fine, fine. It isn't a question of money. It's just, well, after all these years it's gonna feel funny not having the old route any more.

LAURA. What does your wife think?

MACE. Not much. She's gone.

LAURA. Dead?

MACE. She left me about five years ago.

LAURA. I didn't know that.

MACE. Well, you don't go around broadcasting those kinds of things.

LAURA. My goodness, you aren't wearing a wedding band anymore. I never noticed. That was the first thing I looked for when I met you. It was so long ago I'm not sure whether I was interested or whether it was just a nervous habit.

MACE. I haven't been wearing it for a long time.

LAURA. I'm very sorry.

MACE. She just didn't like being married anymore. That

happens to some couples. There wasn't anything I could do about it. She's somewhere in California now, "Getting her shit together," was the way she put it. Her last few months with me she started using expressions like that.

LAURA. She sounds very confused. California might just be the place for her. You know what they say? Two minuses make a plus.

MACE. I hope so. *(A beat)* I liked being married. When it was right, it was terrific.

LAURA. I was never married but I did live with someone for a long time. Then when he went and married someone else it kind of put a damper on the romance.

MACE. Not a very nice guy.

LAURA. Actually, he was a nice guy. It just proves you don't have to be married for a relationship to go sour.

MACE. I don't know why you and I never talked more. Now that we won't be seeing each other I wish we had. I mean, we talked about the weather and the roads and the company, but we never talked about ourselves.

LAURA. Well, I'm five feet four, unattached, Episcopalian, and I love country and western music. If you want my age, that may be a problem.

MACE. It all sounds terrific to me.

LAURA. This is good coffee.

MACE. I'm glad you like it. I grind my own beans. You make a nice sandwich. Tuna fish?

LAURA. Chicken salad.

MACE. Oh, I'm sorry.

LAURA. Don't be. I got it from the machine. It does taste like tuna fish. I like tuna fish. That's why I buy the chicken salad.

MACE. What does the tuna salad taste like?

LAURA. A lot like what your ex-wife is trying to get together in California.

MACE. Damn it, I'm gonna miss this job. It's just like the way it was in the Navy. I hated the Navy. I joined to get away from home, but then when I was out for a couple of years, I actually missed it.

LAURA. Do you miss it now? The Navy, I mean?

MACE. No, not a bit.

LAURA. Too bad. Maybe you could have re-enlisted.

MACE. You've got some sense of humor. I like that…So, any idea what you're gonna do now?

LAURA. No. I've made no plans.

MACE. A cousin of mine owns a dry cleaning shop. He wants me to come work there.

LAURA. Big mistake.

MACE. You think so?

LAURA. Two things you don't do in this world. Jump from tall bridges and work for relatives.

MACE. I really wasn't going to. I've got this camper. My wife always hated it. What I really want to do is take off for about three or four weeks and see the whole country. Maybe do a little fishing, too,

LAURA. Well, then, that's what you should do.

MACE. The country's changing so fast. Building, building, building. It's getting to be wall to wall shopping centers. Pretty soon anything worth seeing will be gone. I really feel sorry for the generations after us. They're gonna miss a lot. I never saw what my father saw and…

LAURA. And your kids, if you have any, will never see what you saw.

MACE. *(A beat)* I did have one. A boy. Tommy. Lost him in a car accident. About ten years ago. I think that's really why she left. She got all screwed up after Tommy died.

LAURA. That's too bad. That's probably when you needed each other the most.

MACE. We should have had more children, but we didn't. Not everyone handles things the same way. The marriage just kept getting worse. There was nothing I could do about it. It was kind'a lonely after she left. It still is.

(An awkward beat)

Look, I'm not a bad guy. I'm neat, I can cook, barbecue, and I'm not that set in my ways. I've been thinking, I've been thinking about it longer than you'd imagine. Laura, maybe you and I could…

LAURA. I can't, Mace. I know what you're gonna ask. You'd like me to go with you. It sounds like a good idea, but I can't.

MACE. You've got someone else?

LAURA. No. No one.

MACE. I'm scared, Laura. When I had the bus to drive, I was fine. I knew what was expected of me and I did it. But now that's gone. I've got no direction, no one, nothing to point the way any more. It may seem strange, but right now I feel closer to you than anyone else. Sure, maybe we didn't talk to each other very much, but maybe we didn't have to. We still knew each other and I think we would get along real fine. Real fine.

LAURA. I know we would, Mace. I know it, too.

MACE. Then what's stopping you? What's stopping you from saying the hell with everything and going off with me? What's to stop us from behaving like silly little school kids and take a fling at life?

LAURA. I'm in chemotherapy, Mace.

MACE. *(A beat)* Oh, no.

LAURA. Goddamn lungs. Goddamn cigarettes.

MACE. Bad?

LAURA. Let's put it this way. I'm not going to have much use for next year's calendar.

MACE. Oh, no, Laura.

LAURA. I guess I asked for it. I smoked for years. My mother got away with it. My sisters got away with it. But I didn't. A stupid tiny little spot on the lung. Damn funny coincidence, isn't it? Me and the bus station going out of business about the same time.

MACE. I don't know what to say.

LAURA. You don't have to say anything but I really appreciate the invitation. I really do.

MACE. Look, there's no reason we still can't...

LAURA. We can't, Mace. I don't want to. It isn't fair. Not to me, not to you. I've got no real attachments now, so I can just go out with no regrets. But if I begin to mean something to you and you begin to mean something to me, then we're both gonna suffer. I know it sounds crazy but I'd just like to leave without regrets, Mace. I really want to.

MACE. I'm sick about this, Laura. I gotta do something. I want to do something.

LAURA. You can, Mace. You can go on and not be afraid of life, the way I'm not afraid of death. Maybe I just have a sick sense of humor, Mace, but maybe we can look at it like we're both going someplace nice. We're both going to take trips that we really want to take. And let's enjoy them and not be afraid. That's what I want most of all. And you know what?

(*She puts her hand on his*)

I'm gonna say "hi" to Tommy for you. I promise.

(*Mace bows his head*)

(*The LIGHTS SLOWLY FADE OUT and then SLOWLY COME UP again. The Bus Station is now dimly lit except for the playing areas.* **JUNE**, *the young bride, is seated on the bench, waiting. She is still in her wedding gown.* **AL**, *the cop, ENTERS from street*)

AL. Is this where we wait?

JUNE. Yes. There should be a bus coming for us soon.

AL. (*Looks around*) The Bus Station. I have to admit it's appropriate for the end of the line.

JUNE. Symbolic, I would say. I love symbolic things, don't you?

AL. I guess they're okay.

JUNE. Well, to me, symbolism is very meaningful. I guess that's why I love foreign movies. Especially the ones dubbed in English. I hate when you have to read all that stuff on the bottom of the screen, don't you? I do.

AL. *(Puzzled)* Yeah. I guess.

(Sits down)

I see you were a bride when your number came up.

JUNE. Yes. It was a real fluke. We were coming out of the church and the huge cross on top of the steeple fell on me.

AL. Now that's symbolic.

JUNE. Really? I wasn't that certain. But still for lightning to strike a cross on a beautiful summer day is a bit unusual. How did you get here?

AL. Nothing out of the ordinary. A maniac with a gun.

JUNE. Oh, no. I hate those kind of people, don't you? Was he caught?

AL. Sure, but with plea bargaining, his attorney got the charges reduced to operating a motor vehicle without a license. He got out of jail before I was buried.

JUNE. Justice is just not fair, is it?

AL. It makes you wonder.

JUNE. Well, when it's not fair, they ought to call it something else.

AL. *(Looks at her curiously)* The guy you married is a very lucky man.

*(**MACE**, the bus driver, ENTERS from street, rubbing his chest)*

MACE. Boy, oh boy, was that some cardiac arrest. Who ever thought I'd go like that?

AL. Death is full of surprises.

MACE. Tell me about it. I was driving along in my camper through the Rockies, when I heard this terrible bang, kind of like a blowout. Naturally, I thought it was a tire. Was I surprised to find out it was me. By the way, I'm Mace.

JUNE. I'm June.

AL. I'm Al.

MACE. Glad to know you. Been here long?

JUNE. I don't know. My Rolex is at the jewelers.

AL. I just got here.

MACE. I never would have believed I'd be back in a bus station. I expected something like a silver cloud or maybe a big bright room with a lot of gold and marble.

JUNE. I just hope we get halos and wings and can fly wherever we want.

AL. I have a feeling you were able to do that before you died.

MACE. How long do you think we'll have to wait here?

AL. I have no idea.

MACE. Well, maybe I can use the time to figure out what it was all about.

JUNE. What "what" was all about?

MACE. Life.

JUNE. I haven't the foggiest.

AL. That doesn't surprise me.

JUNE. Don't get me wrong, I really liked it. All the wonderful things you can buy, it's just unbelievable. Of course I know I was shallow and vain and a bit of a scatterbrain, but eventually I would have caught on. That's what my mother told Arnold anyway. Actually that's the beauty of being young. You're never bothered whether life is about something or not. That's a topic you save to discuss with your therapist when you're in your forties. What I really want to find out about is tornadoes. I never did understand what purpose they served, did you?

MACE. Bad news. You can still get headaches after you're dead.

AL. Well, I'm kind of glad it's all over.

MACE. Really?

AL. Yeah, being a cop became too confusing. The rules

seemed to get too blurry. Wrong wasn't necessarily wrong and right wasn't necessarily right and somehow we stopped being heroes for a lot of people. Suddenly, doing my best, trying to keep the streets safe, wasn't what it was all about. It got so I couldn't figure out who were the good guys and who were the bad guys.

MACE. I hated all the new complicated technical advancements they kept coming up with. There were some nights I actually couldn't sleep wondering just how obsolete all that cyber space crap made me.

JUNE. I got sheets up the gazoo at my shower.

(Mace and Al stare at her in amazement)

MACE. Sheets?

JUNE. Well, when you talked about not being able to sleep, it just reminded me about all the great gifts I got at my shower. I also got a lot of can openers.

AL. Do you know what you just interrupted? We are talking heavy things here. We are talking about life and its meaning.

JUNE. I know. I was just trying to change the subject to something less complicated.

*(The **BAG LADY** ENTERS from street with a shopping bag)*

BAG LADY. Hi, how's it going?

(She finds an old paper and puts it in her bag)

MACE. Fine.

JUNE. Fantastic.

AL. Not bad.

BAG LADY. *(Notices a magazine next to **MACE**)* Is that your magazine?

MACE. No, no, it was here. You can have it.

BAG LADY. *(Puts the magazine in her shopping bag)* Thanks. It's hard to break a habit even when you're not living any more.

(Sits down)

Pheww! Talk about having a bad day. I mean you see a sign on the street that says "One Way" with an arrow pointing to the right. So what do you do when you cross? You look left, right? So I cross, looking left, and a truck from the right backs over me, right? That's how I left. Did I need that? God, I didn't want to go.

AL. Why not? You certainly don't look like you had it so easy.

BAG LADY. Are you kidding? I loved living. Do you know the thrill I got finding a copy of Good Housekeeping with none of the recipes torn out? Or the joy of going through a trash can and coming up with an issue of Oprah that I hadn't read at my chiropractor's office? This very month I found eight books about Financial Planning. I almost finished reading the fourth one and guess what? I was doing everything right.

MACE. That made you happy? Something as simple as sifting through a bunch of rubbish and finding old magazines and books?

BAG LADY. Well, I never cared to travel and jewelry didn't do a thing for me. Listen, who's to say what should or shouldn't make people happy, but when something does, that's what it's all about.

MACE. I don't buy into that happiness bag. That's too easy. Some of us had some tough times.

BAG LADY. Who doesn't? Remember that last newspaper strike? I walked around for weeks with half empty shopping bags. Talk about depression. Anyway, I maintain that nothing is the end of the world...except maybe this. And as long as you were breathing in and out you had a shot at something, a nice afternoon, a good laugh, maybe even someone to hold your hand. And whenever one of those things came along, I'd say thank you very much. Thank you very, very much.

JUNE. You're an upbeat person. I like you. So what else was it all about just in case we're asked questions?

BAG LADY. Life was about everything. It was about kindness, charity, love, hope, new shoes, warm coats, health, illness, crime, punishment and religion, and exactly in that order.

AL. I guess it was too screwed up to be about only one thing.

BAG LADY. Yes, but it gave us choices. We could pick what we wanted from it.

JUNE. My favorite things were getting a suntan and kissing.

AL. I liked hot apple pie, especially that first bite.

JUNE. That's right. And you only had to eat a small piece to know how good the whole pie tasted.

MACE. If only I could have gotten closer to someone, or believed in something, that might have done it for me. I loved holding my boy. I can still remember it. It was wonderful.

BAG LADY. Well, you had that so you didn't leave empty handed. That would be the shame of it all, to leave with nothing, wouldn't it?

MACE. *(Rises while thinking about it)* Yeah…Yeah, holding my boy. I guess I did have something.

AL. I was married to a woman who got along with my mother. That was a bit of luck.

JUNE. I had Arnold and my parents and, do dogs count? I had the cutest little cocker spaniel who sat on my lap and went through all the mail order catalogues with me.

BAG LADY. You bet dogs count. I remember my first puppy as a kid. How he always licked my face. I never had to use a napkin.

MACE. Maybe we all had something. If only we took the time to think about it when we were there. Ahhh, who are we kidding? We're all going to miss life.

JUNE. Maybe that's good. Maybe missing life means we had one.

AL. Guess what? For the first time since I met you, you make sense.

JUNE. Really? Darn it! There's no one here I know to see that.

STATION MASTER (V.O.) Attention! Attention! Last Bus now boarding at Gate Number One.

AL. Did he say last bus?

MACE. I have a feeling that's what they're all called here.

AL. He didn't tell us where we're headed.

JUNE. Are you afraid?

AL. *(Rising)* I'm not sure. Suddenly I don't like the idea that there may not be anything more.

JUNE. *(Rising)* Would you like me to hold your hand? It always helps when I'm scared.

AL. *(A beat)* You know, I'd like that. I really would.

MACE. *(To **BAG LADY**)* And I'll hold yours. Hey, just the fact that we still feel a need for each other is a hopeful sign, isn't it?

JUNE. I think it is.

AL. Yeah, I think so, too.

BAG LADY. Well, onward and let's hope upward.

*(They are about to go when **MACE**, noticing the audience, steps out to address them)*

MACE. And for the privilege of passing through, thank you. Thank you very much.

BAG LADY. *(She also steps out to audience)* Thank you. Thank you very much.

AL. *(Also stepping out to audience)* Thank you. Thank you very much.

JUNE. *(Also stepping out to audience)* Thank you. Thank you very much.

(The actors are now all facing the audience. They bow their heads)

THE STAGE GOES DARK

THE END

PROPS

ACT I

WAITING
Newspaper
2 briefcases
Pocket change

BABY FEET FRANK.
Gun

OLD FRIENDS
2 shopping bags filled with old clothes and trash
Several newspapers and magazines
Small suitcase
Pack of cigarettes
5 Bic Cigarette lighters
Small tin Altoid box
Coins for vending machine
Paper cup from coffee vending machine
Pen and small pad of paper
A Central High School Sweater for Fred that will match the Bag Lady's
Several folded plastic hotel laundry bags

A BETTER WORLD
Small whisk broom
Briefcase
Newspaper
Ladies soft handbag
Wallet
Police night stick

ACT II

HERE'S HARRY
Small package *(shoe box size)* wrapped in black
Small, unwrapped gift box containing a woman's bracelet

THE HAPPIEST BRIDE
2 bus tickets
Cell phone

WITHOUT REGRETS
Thermos with coffee
Sandwich from vending machine
Coffee mug

LAST BUS
Shopping bag from "Old Friends" scene
A newspaper and magazine

COSTUMES

ACT I

WAITING
Walter – Suit and tie
Jane – Skirt, blouse and cardigan sweater
Howard – Suit and tie
Lorraine – Coat, house coat, curlers, house slippers

BABY FEET FRANK.
Frank – Turtle neck sweater and slacks
Clara – Skirt and blouse
Bus Driver – Bus driver uniform and cap

OLD FRIENDS
Bag Lady – Hat, ragged old coat, high school sweater, baggy dress, baggy socks, high top sneakers
Fred – Sport coat, slacks, sport shirt

A BETTER WORLD
Audrey – Jacket, blouse and skirt
Ernest – Suit and tie, watch
Marsha – Dress
Al – Cop Uniform and cap

ACT II

HERE'S HARRY
Mrs. Evans – Black Dress, black purse
Mr. Wade – Black suit, white shirt, black tie

THE HAPPIEST BRIDE
June – Wedding dress and veil, large diamond ring, bridal garter belt
Bobby – Jeans, t-shirt, sneakers

WITHOUT REGRETS
Mace – Bus Driver uniform and cap
Laura – Dark sweater, skirt

LAST BUS
June – Wedding dress and veil from "The Happiest Bride" scene
Al – Cop uniform and cap from "A Better World" scene
Mace – Slacks, flannel shirt
Bag Lady – Same outfit from "Old Friends" scene

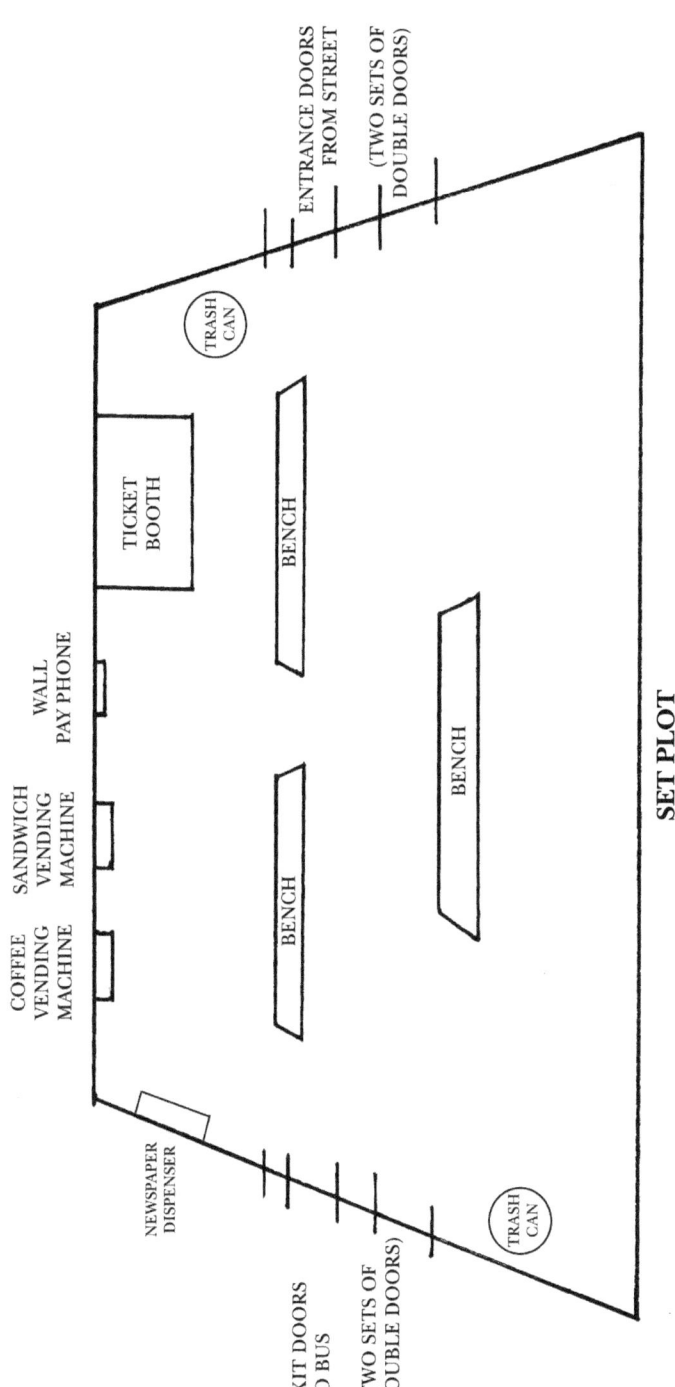

From the Reviews of
PASSENGERS...

"For a real adventure in theatre, hop on board *Passengers*...[It] is a fresh, idiosyncratic, irreverent comedy set in, of all places, a bus station. In eight sketches, a series of characters meet in the bus station. The encounters weave together a subtle but profound theme...*Passengers* is a great script. The characters are good and the dialog witty and sharp...Everything about this show is unexpected and unconventional."
– *Niles Daily Times*

Also by
Sam Bobrick...

Annoyance
Are You Sure?
Baggage
The Crazy Time
Death in England
Flemming (An American Thriller)
Getting Sara Married
Hamlet II (Better Than the Original)
Last Chance Romance
Murder at the Howard Johnson's
New York Water
No Hard Feelings
Norman, Is That You?
The Outrageous Adventures of
Sheldon and Mrs. Levine
Remember Me?
Splitting Issues
The Stanway Case
Wally's Cafe
Weekend Comedy

Please visit our website **samuelfrench.com** for complete
descriptions and licensing information

OTHER TITLES AVAILABLE FROM SAMUEL FRENCH

FEMININE ENDING
Sarah Treem

Full Length / Dark Comedy / 3m, 2f / Various, Unit set
Amanda, twenty-five, wants to be a great composer. But at the moment, she's living in New York City and writing advertising jingles to pay the rent while her fiancée, Jack pursues his singing career. So when Amanda's mother, Kim, calls one evening from New Hampshire and asks for her help with something she can't discuss over the phone, Amanda is only too happy to leave New York. Once home, Kim reveals that she's leaving Amanda father and needs help packing. Amanda balks and ends up (gently) hitting the postman, who happens to be her first boyfriend. They spend the night together in an apple orchard, where Amanda tries to tell Billy how her life got sidetracked. It has something to do with being a young woman in a profession that only recognizes famous men. Billy acts like he might have the answer, but doesn't. Neither does Amanda's mother. Or, for that matter, her father. A Feminine Ending is a gentle, bittersweet comedy about a girl who knows what she wants but not quite how to get it. Her parents are getting divorced, her fiancée is almost famous, her first love reappears, and there's a lot of noise in her head but none of it is music. Until the end.

"Darkly comic. *Feminine Ending* has undeniable wit."
- *New York Post*

"Appealingly outlandish humor."
- *The New York Times*

"Courageous. The 90-minute piece swerves with nerve and naivete. Sarah Treem has a voice all her own."
- *Newsday*

SAMUELFRENCH.COM

OTHER TITLES AVAILABLE FROM SAMUEL FRENCH

MAURITIUS
Theresa Rebeck

Comedy / 3m, 2f / Interior

Stamp collecting is far more risky than you think. After their mother's death, two estranged half-sisters discover a book of rare stamps that may include the crown jewel for collectors. One sister tries to collect on the windfall, while the other resists for sentimental reasons. In this gripping tale, a seemingly simple sale becomes dangerous when three seedy, high-stakes collectors enter the sisters' world, willing to do anything to claim the rare find as their own.

"(Theresa Rebeck's) belated Broadway bow, the only original play by a woman to have its debut on Broadway this fall."
- Robert Simonson, *New York Times*

"*Mauritius* caters efficiently to a hunger that Broadway hasn't been gratifying in recent years. That's the corkscrew-twist drama of suspense… she has strewn her script with a multitude of mysteries."
- Ben Brantley, *New York Times*

"Theresa Rebeck is a slick playwright… Her scenes have a crisp shape, her dialogue pops, her characters swagger through an array of showy emotion, and she knows how to give a plot a cunning twist."
- John Lahr, *The New Yorker*

SAMUELFRENCH.COM